The Not So Good Goat

Little Learners Love Literacy®

Tim ran home from school one day and said,

“Aiden and his Nan are going on a boat trip. Can we keep her goat for a week?”

“A goat?” said Dad with a groan. “That might be tricky.”

No, no. It will eat all the weeds for you.
Oh, all right.

So Dad went down the road

to get the goat.

“Hello,” said Nan.
“This is Joan.
She is a good goat.
I will help you load
her into the van.”

But Dad was right.

Joan the goat was very tricky.

She went

CHOMP

CHOMP

CHOMP

on Dad's old coat.

“Goats like to try things to eat,”

said Mum.

And Joan was very good at jumping. She went over the rails of the pen and tried to climb the oak tree!

Whoa, Joan,
WHOA!
Goats like
to roam and
climb high.

Joan went clip clop clip into the kitchen.

She was eating the toast and munching on the oats!

Whoa, Joan,
WHOA!
Goats must only
have toast for a treat.

Then Joan got on to Tim's bed!

Joan needs
our help.

So Joan got a big pen for roaming, a high hill, lots of yummy weeds to eat and a teeny bit of toast for a treat.

And she was good, most of the time ...

When Nan got back, she said,

Naaaa.

How to use this book

The Little Learners Love Literacy® stories enable children to practise their sound–letter relationship knowledge through reading. Each story is carefully sequenced to give children confidence and success.

Stage 7 Little Learner books focus on:

Vowel sounds: one, two, three or four graphemes representing a vowel sound.

The Not So Good Goat focuses on the vowel sound **/ō/** with **oa** as in **goat**.

Continue to encourage children to 'decode' or 'sound out' any unfamiliar words. To do this, children point to each grapheme and say the sounds; for example, **g**-**oa**-**t** or **f**-**l**-**oa**-**t**. Then they blend these sounds together to read the word. Longer words such as **roaming**, can be broken into two parts to decode: **r-oa-m (roam) + i-ng (ing)**.

Heart words: These are words that children need to 'learn by heart' as they cannot decode them at this stage. Some of the words in the previous books will now be decodable as children have more sound–letter relationship knowledge. Only the new Heart words are listed.

Speed sounds: Children point to each grapheme as they read it.

Questions to talk about: After children have read the book, it is important to talk about the questions and enjoy the story together. These questions help with comprehension and vocabulary. If they wish, children can refer to the book when answering questions.

Speed words: This word list gives children practice reading decodable words with **oa**. Encourage children to 'sound out' each word until they can read it automatically. Repeated reading practice will increase fluency and automaticity.

This Speed word page can be photocopied and the words cut up for further activities:

- Sort the words into groups according to the number of sounds: 2 sounds oa-k; 3 sounds g-oa-t, b-oa-t, r-oa-d, J-oa-n, t-oa-s-t, f-l-oa-t, c-oa-t, c-oa-ch, oa-t-s, r-oa-m, s-oa-p, f-oa-m; 4 sounds b-oa-s-t, c-oa-s-t, r-oa-s-t, g-r-oa-n; 5 sounds r-oa-m-i-ng.
- Play 'A Goat Eating Toast'. Photocopy the Speed words twice. Draw 'a piece of toast' on 36 cards and paste one word on the other side. Shuffle the word cards and deal each child five cards. Place the remaining cards in the middle, tree side up. The aim is to collect pairs of the same word. Children take turns reading one of their words then ask another player if they have its matching pair. If the player has the word, they read it and give it to the other player. If not, the player takes a card from the middle. Continue until all words have been matched.

Heart words

Speed sounds

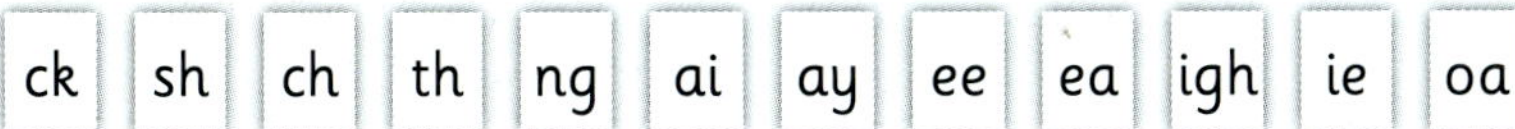

Questions to talk about

- What is the name of the goat?
- How long did Joan have to stay?
- Why was Dad so reluctant?
- How did Tim convince Dad to take the goat?
- What tricky things did Joan do at Tim and Pip's house?
- Find the word that means to 'to move around'. (roam)
- What word does 'naaa' sound like? (No)
- Would **you** tell Nan about the tricky things Joan did?

Speed words

goat	groan	boat
road	Joan	coat
oak	roam	toast
oats	roaming	soap
boast	foam	roast
float	coast	coach